COOL CARS

## ASTON MARTIN
# VALHALLA

BY NATHAN SOMMER

EPIC

BELLWETHER MEDIA ››› MINNEAPOLIS, MN

**EPIC BOOKS** are no ordinary books. They burst with intense action, high-speed heroics, and shadows of the unknown. Are you ready for an Epic adventure?

This edition first published in 2023 by Bellwether Media, Inc.

No part of this publication may be reproduced in whole or in part without written permission of the publisher. For information regarding permission, write to Bellwether Media, Inc., Attention: Permissions Department, 6012 Blue Circle Drive, Minnetonka, MN 55343.

Library of Congress Cataloging-in-Publication Data

LC record for Aston Martin Valhalla available at: https://lccn.loc.gov/2022020248

Text copyright © 2023 by Bellwether Media, Inc. EPIC and associated logos are trademarks and/or registered trademarks of Bellwether Media, Inc.

Editor: Kieran Downs    Series Designer: Jeffrey Kollock    Book Designer: Josh Brink

Printed in the United States of America, North Mankato, MN

# TABLE OF CONTENTS

| | |
|---|---|
| LIGHTNING QUICK | 4 |
| ALL ABOUT THE VALHALLA | 6 |
| PARTS OF THE VALHALLA | 12 |
| THE VALHALLA'S FUTURE | 20 |
| GLOSSARY | 22 |
| TO LEARN MORE | 23 |
| INDEX | 24 |

# LIGHTNING QUICK ≫

A crowd gathers. The Aston Martin Valhalla is here! This brand-new car is a sight to see.

The crowd checks out the car's features. This **hybrid** car looks like it is from the future!

# ALL ABOUT THE VALHALLA »

**1921 ASTON HILL CLIMB**

Aston Martin began in London, England, in 1913. The company won the 1914 **Aston Hill Climb**.

Aston Martins are known for comfort. They are also fast. Famous cars include the DB5, V8 Vantage, and DBS.

ASTON MARTIN DB5

The Aston Martin Valhalla was first shown in 2019. This hybrid sports car is built to be like **Formula 1** race cars.

The Valhalla is a road build of Aston Martin's Valkyrie race car. It is nicknamed "son of Valkyrie."

**VALKYRIE AMR PRO**

**VALHALLA**

# VALHALLA BASICS

**YEAR FIRST MADE** 2023

**COST** starts at $800,000

**HOW MANY MADE** 999

### FEATURES

doors that open upwards  | wide grille  | large rear wing

The Valhalla is made in Gaydon, England. It runs on both gasoline and **electricity**.

The car hits top speeds of 217 miles (349 kilometers) per hour!

# PARTS OF THE VALHALLA

The Valhalla has a powerful **V8 engine**. It also has a plug-in **powertrain**. This allows it to be powered by **battery** for a short time.

## ENGINE SPECS

TWIN-TURBO 4.0-LITER V8

TOP SPEED: 217 miles (349 kilometers) per hour

0-60 TIME: 2.5 seconds

HORSEPOWER: 937 hp

The car can reach speeds of 80 miles (129 kilometers) per hour in electric mode.

The Valhalla's body is made of **carbon fiber**. A wide **grille** covers most of the front.

A large rear **wing** helps the car cut through wind. Its doors open upwards for easy entry.

The Valhalla's seats connect to its **chassis**. Raised **footwells** give it the feel of a race car.

### A WINNING IDEA

Formula 1 driver Sebastian Vettel helped make the Valhalla. He is a four-time world champion.

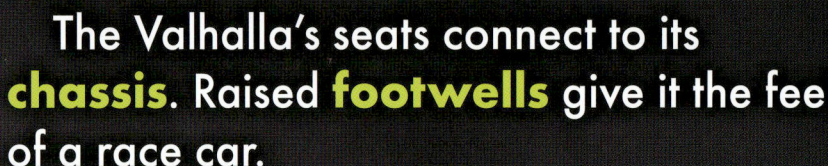

SEBASTIAN VETTEL

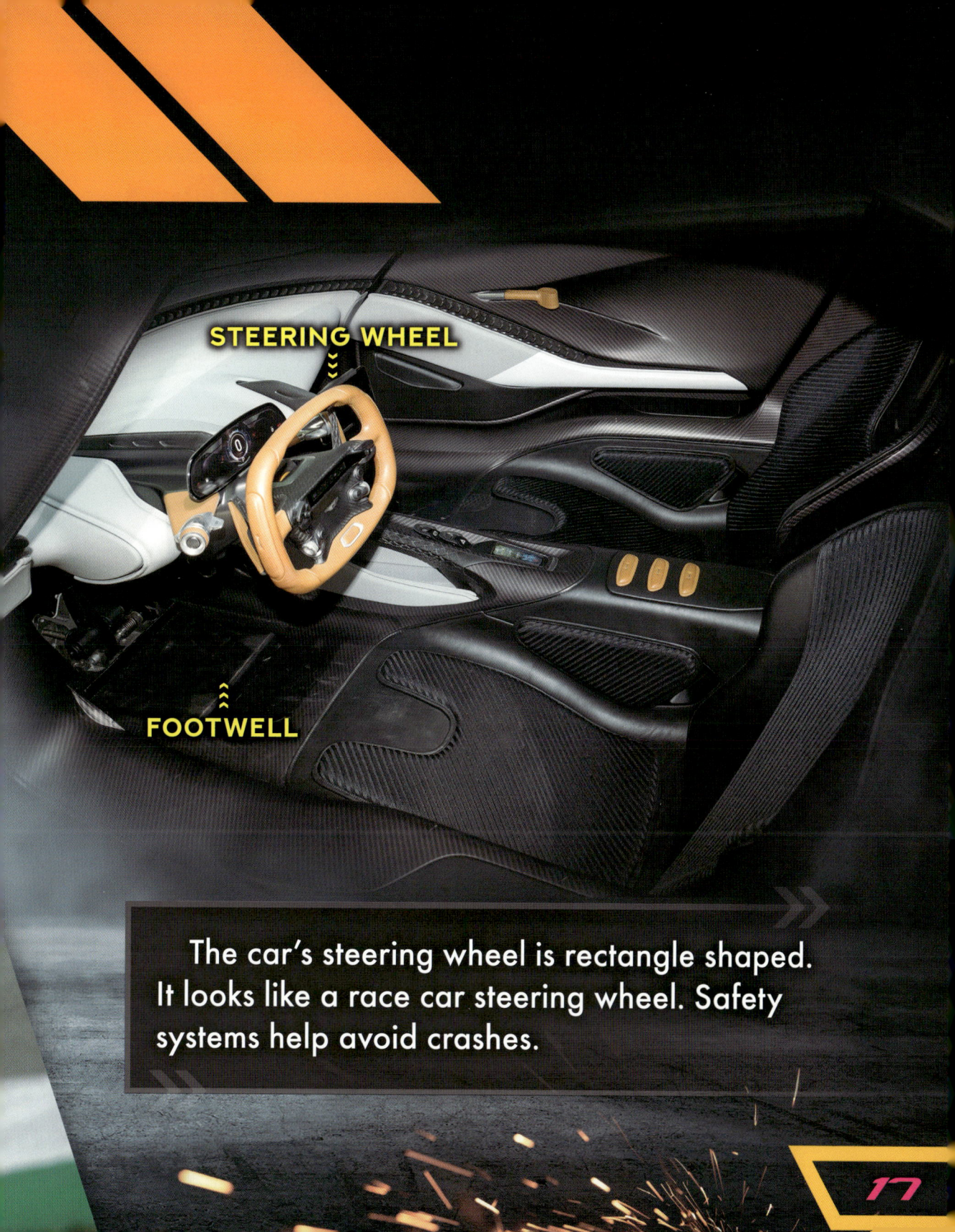

**STEERING WHEEL**

**FOOTWELL**

The car's steering wheel is rectangle shaped. It looks like a race car steering wheel. Safety systems help avoid crashes.

17

The Valhalla's **suspension system** helps its tires grip the road. This creates a smooth ride. The suspension can also change with the road. The car's front raises when it goes up hills.

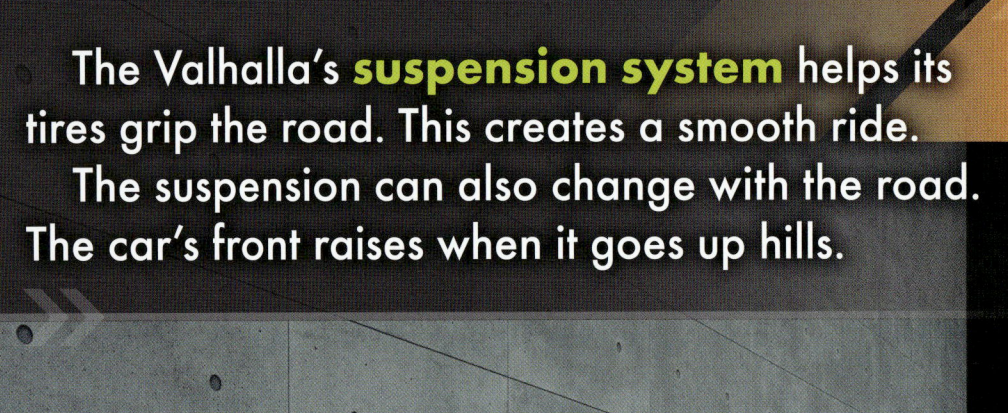

**RED BULL RACING**

The Red Bull Racing team helped make the Valhalla's body.

# THE VALHALLA'S FUTURE >>

The Valhalla is one of Aston Martin's first hybrid cars. The company will make more hybrids soon. They also plan to make fully electric cars. Aston Martin has a bright, electric future!

**BOND'S FAVORITE CAR**

Aston Martins have been in many James Bond movies. The Valhalla was in 2021's *No Time to Die*.

# GLOSSARY

**Aston Hill Climb**—a car race held in Buckinghamshire, England, from 1904 until 1925

**battery**—a part that supplies electric energy to a car

**carbon fiber**—a strong, lightweight material made from woven pieces of carbon

**chassis**—the bottom part of a car that holds up its body

**electricity**—power that is carried through wires and is used to run machines

**footwells**—the spaces for feet in front of a car's seats

**Formula 1**—a type of car racing

**grille**—a set of bars that cover an opening on the front of a car; the grille allows air to enter and exit the engine.

**hybrid**—using both a gasoline engine and an electric motor for power

**powertrain**—a system in a car that delivers power to the driving wheels

**suspension system**—a series of parts that help a car grip the road and move more smoothly over bumps

**V8 engine**—an engine with eight cylinders arranged in the shape of a "V"

**wing**—a part on a car's body that helps it travel smoothly through the air at high speeds

# TO LEARN MORE

## AT THE LIBRARY

Albino, Dustin. *Superfast Formula 1 Racing*. Minneapolis, Minn.: Lerner Publications, 2020.

Rea, Amy C. *Aston Martin DB9*. Minnetonka, Minn.: Kaleidoscope, 2019.

Smith, Ryan. *Aston Martin*. New York, N.Y.: AV2, 2021.

## ON THE WEB

Factsurfer.com gives you a safe, fun way to find more information.

1. Go to www.factsurfer.com.

2. Enter "Aston Martin Valhalla" into the search box and click 🔍.

3. Select your book cover to see a list of related content.

# INDEX

Aston Hill Climb, 6
basics, 9
battery, 12
body, 14, 19
chassis, 16
company, 6, 8, 20
doors, 15
electricity, 10, 13, 20
engine, 12
engine specs, 12
footwells, 16, 17
Formula 1, 8, 16
gasoline, 10
Gaydon, England, 10, 11
grille, 14
history, 6, 8
hybrid, 5, 8, 20

London, England, 6
models, 7, 8
movies, 21
powertrain, 12
racing, 6, 8, 16, 17, 19
Red Bull Racing, 19
safety systems, 17
seats, 16
speeds, 10, 13
steering wheel, 17
suspension system, 18
Vettel, Sebastian, 16
wing, 15

The images in this book are reproduced through the courtesy of: Matti Blume/ Wiki Commons, front cover (hero), p. 9 (Valhalla); Norikazu, front cover (background); Alexander Migl/ Wiki Commons, p. 3; Bloomberg/ Getty Images, pp. 4, 5, 13, 14, 15, 17; Motoring Picture Library/ Alamy, p. 6; Uli Jooss/ Alamy, p. 7; Alexandre Prévot/ Wiki Commons, pp. 8-9; auto-data.net, pp. 9 (door, grille, wing), 12; Bascar, pp. 10, 11, 18; Marco Canoniero/ Alamy, p. 16; SPTNK/ AP images, p. 19; Owen Humphreys/ Alamy, p. 20; David Williams/ Alamy, p. 21.